NATIONAL GEOGRAPHIC
Reach™
Language • Literacy • Content

NATIONAL GEOGRAPHIC LEARNING | CENGAGE Learning

Contents

Unit 3: Visit the Farm!

Unit 4: All Kinds of Plants

Unit 5: Wind, Rain, and Snow

Unit 6: It's Our Town

Unit 7: On the Job

Unit 8: Sun, Moon, Stars Above

Name _____

Unit Concept Map

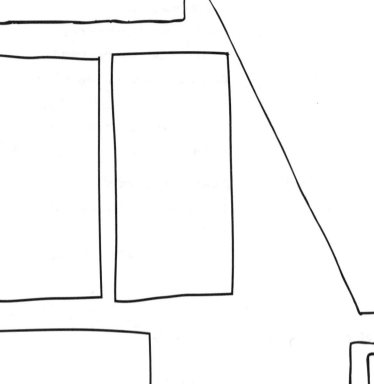
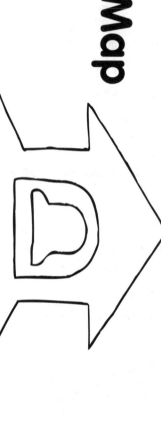

Directions: Have children draw pictures of things that they do at school in each box.

For use with TE p. T7

1.1

Unit 1 | Step into School

Name _____

School Tools

block

book

crayon

pencil

glue

scissors

Directions: Have children color the school tools. Then have them play a game with a partner. One partner chooses a tool and pantomimes using the tool. The other partner guesses the tool.

Name _____

Story Map

Beginning:

Middle:

End:

Directions: Help children add illustrations that show what happens in *A Great First Day*.

1.3

Name _____

Vocabulary

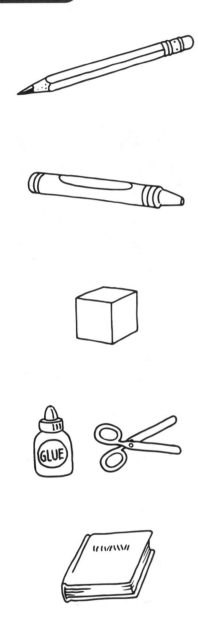

make

read

run

write

draw

build

Directions: Have children draw a line that connects the picture of the school tool with the picture that shows the action. Then have them play a game with a partner. One partner chooses an action to act out and the other partner guesses the action.

Name _____

School Places

classroom

lunch room

bathroom

office

playground

bus stop

Directions: Say the two school places in a row. Then choose one of the places and direct children to color that place. Repeat for each row. Then have partners play a game. One partner should choose a place and act out something you can do there. The other partner should guess the place.

Writing

Plan Sentences

Name _____

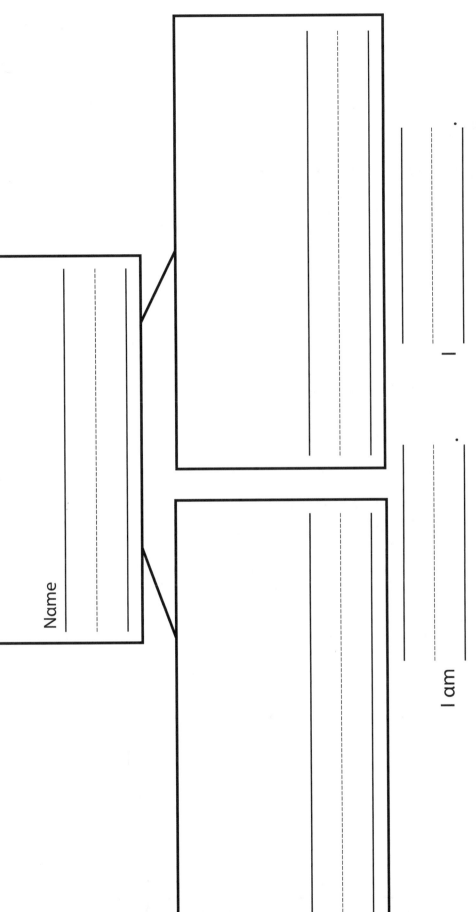

I am _____ .

I _____ .

Directions: Have children write their name in the top box. Then have them write or draw things they do in the other boxes. Help them complete the sentences by writing their name in the first frame and then writing an action word telling something they can do in the second frame.

For use with TE p. T65 and p. T69

1.6

Unit 1 | Step into School

Name _____

Compare Pictures

Different

Same

Directions: Guide children through completing each part of the graphic organizer. Have children write or draw a way that the pictures in *Keisha Ann Can!* and "Places in My School" are the same and different. Provide help as needed.

Writing

All About Me!

I am _____ .

I _____ .

I _____ .

Directions: Day 3: Have children draw a picture of themselves. Then help children draft their informational sentences. Remind them to use their ideas from **Practice Master 1.6**. Day 4: Have children revise and edit their sentences by adding more details and checking for capitalization.

Name _____

School Commands

sit

stand

ask

point

share

bring

Directions: Say the two commands in the row. Have children draw a line to match each command to its picture. Then have partners play a game. Have one partner say a command and the other partner do the action.

Name _____

All About Me!

I am _____.

I _____.

I _____.

Directions: Have children copy their sentences. Remind them to leave some space between each word. Have children draw a picture to match their sentences.

Name _____

Unit Concept Map

FAMILY

FUN

Directions: Add your ideas to the concept map.

Name _____

Family

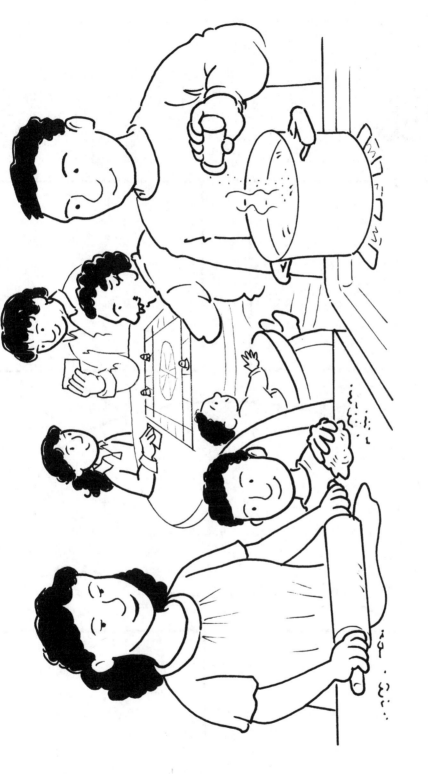

baby   brother   father   grandma   grandpa   sister   mother

Directions: Have children color the pictures. Read each word aloud. Then have children draw a line from the word to the correct family member.

Name _____

Idea Web

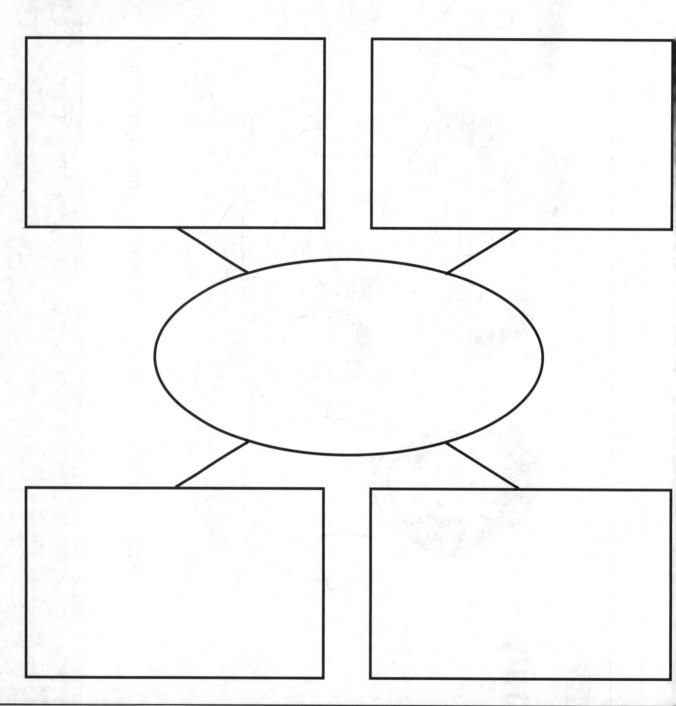

Directions: Have children write or draw the main idea and details from *Tab and Her Family*. Show the main idea in the center oval and the details in the boxes.

Name _____

Food Words

1.

pizza

fish

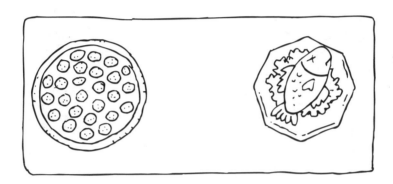

2.

salad

rice

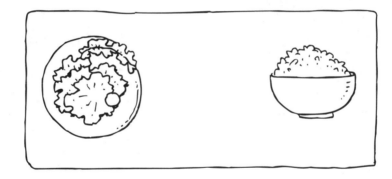

3.

soup

tortillas

Directions: For box 1, read the words and have children follow along. Then have students circle the word *fish* and color the picture of the fish. Repeat with *salad* and *soup* for boxes 2 and 3.

Name _____

Actions

eat

cook

sing

dance

play

laugh

Directions: Have children color the pictures. Then have them play a game with a partner. One partner chooses an action and acts it out. The other partner points to the action on the page or names it.

Name _____

Plan an Invitation

Four-Ws Chart

Who?
What?
Where?
When?

Directions: Help children complete the chart by answering the questions.

Name _____

Compare

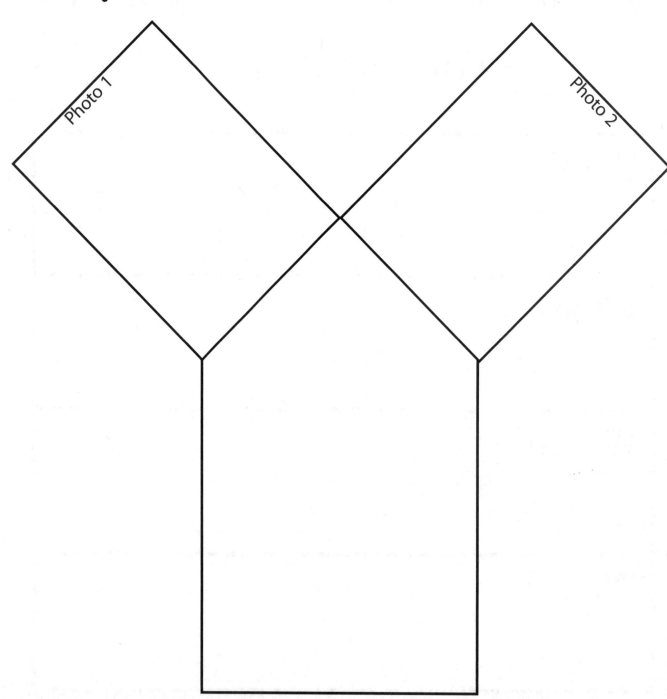

Photo 1

Photo 2

Directions: Have children draw a picture or write key words about the photo in *Gio and His Family* in the top left box. Have children draw a picture or write key words about the photo in "A Tasty Treat" in the top right box. Have children show or write how the photos are alike in the bottom box.

For use with TE p. T161   **2.7**   Unit 2 | My Family and Me

Name _____

Draft an Invitation

_____

Dear _____ .

_____

Please come to my _____ !

_____

Place: _____

_____

Date: _____

_____

Time: _____

Directions: *Day 3* Help children draft their invitations. Remind them to use their chart from **Practice Master 2.6**. *Day 4* Have children revise their letter to invite a second friend or family member. Remind them to check end punctuation.

Name _____

Feeling Words

bored

excited

surprised

angry

Directions: Read aloud each word. Have children look at each set of pictures and circle the picture that best describes the feeling word. Then have children color the pictures.

Name _____

Dear _____,

Please come to my

_____

_____

Place: _____

Date: _____

Time: _____

Directions: Have children copy their invitations. Remind them to leave a little space between letters and more space between words.

Unit Concept Map

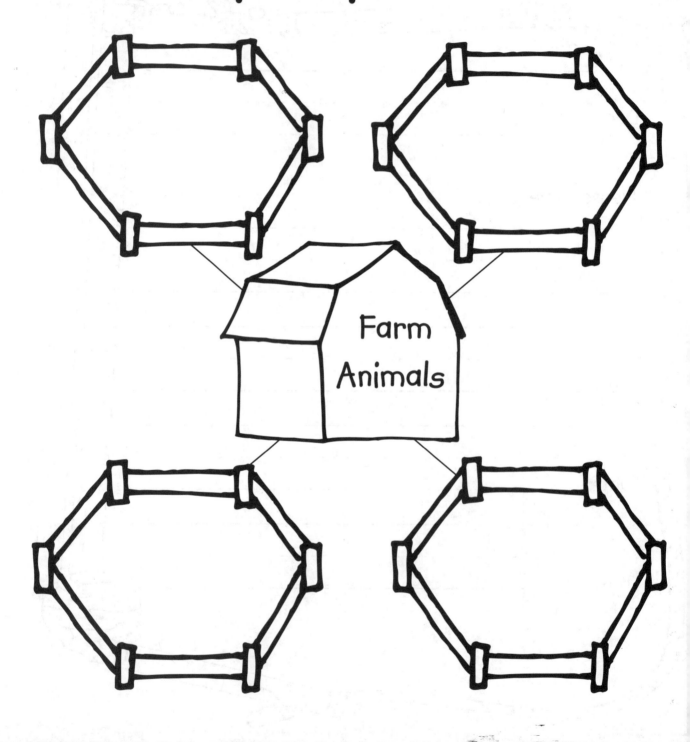

Farm Animals

Name _____

Farm Animals

horse

cow

goat

sheep

pig

duck

chicken

goose

Directions: Have children color the animals. Then have them play a game with a partner. Have one partner choose an animal and act it out. Have the other partner guess the animal.

Name

Sequence Chain

First

Next

Then

Last

3.3

Name _____

Describing Words

①

big

little

②

loud

quiet

③

slow

fast

Directions: For box 1, have children circle the word *big* for and color the animal that is big. Continue with boxes 2 and 3, having children circle the word and color the animal that is *loud* and *fast*.

Name _____

Baby Animals

piglet

calf

foal

duckling

kid

chick

Directions: Have children color the animals. Then have children trace the key words. Choose volunteers to say the name of each animal to the class.

Writing

Plan Informational Sentences

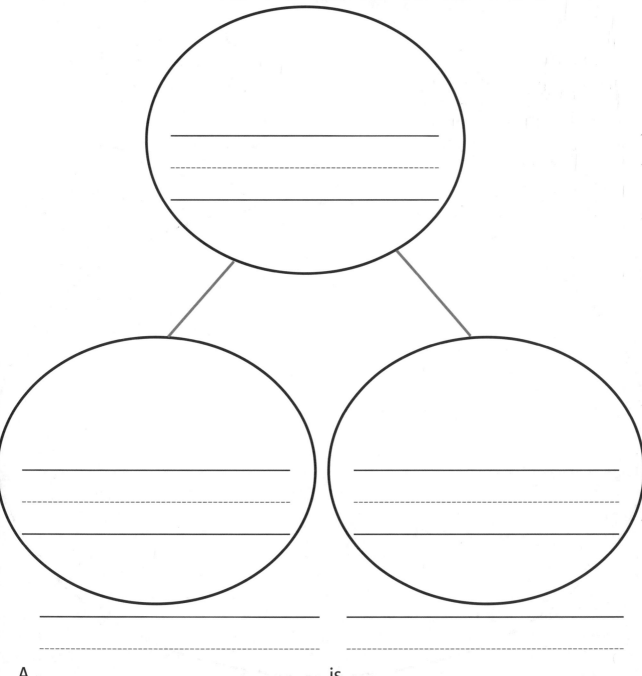

A _____ is _____ .

Directions: Have children write the name of a farm animal in the top circle, and write describing words in the other circles. Have them illustrate the words. Then help them complete the sentence with the animal name and one of the describing words.

3.6

Little Bat and Tiny Bee

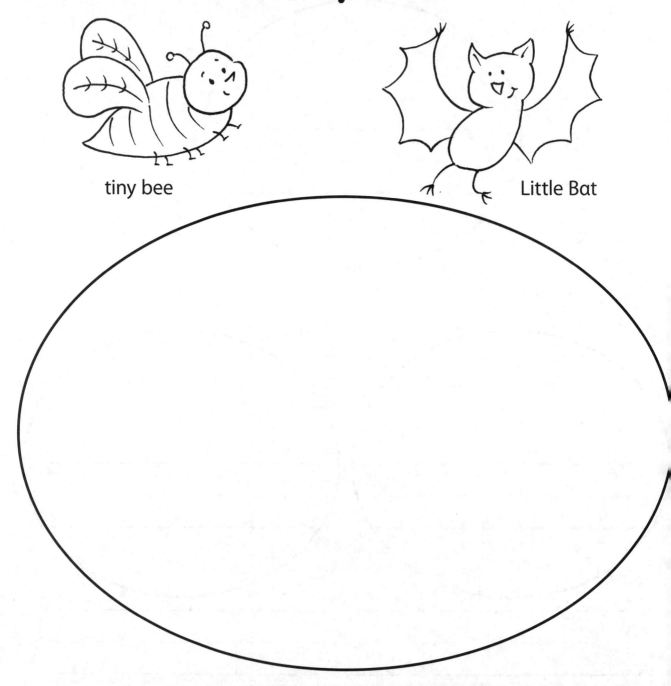

tiny bee

Little Bat

Directions: Talk with children about the ways in which tiny bee and Little Bat are alike. Have children choose one idea to draw in the oval.

Name _____

A _____ is _____ .

A _____ is _____ .

Directions: Day 3: Have children use their idea webs from **Practice Master 3.6** to draw a picture and complete the sentences. Day 4: Have children revise and edit their sentences. Remind them to check capitalization and end punctuation.

Name _____

Animal Parts

horse

duck

Directions: Have children color each animal body part. For example, say: *Look at the horse. Color the tail brown.* Then have children work in pairs to point to and name the feet, legs, head, tail, and wings on the animals.

Name _____

Publish and Share Informational Sentences

_____

Directions: Have children copy their sentences. Remind them to leave a little space between letters and more space between words.

For use with TE p. T261   **3.10**   **Unit 3** | Visit the Farm!

Name

Unit Concept Map

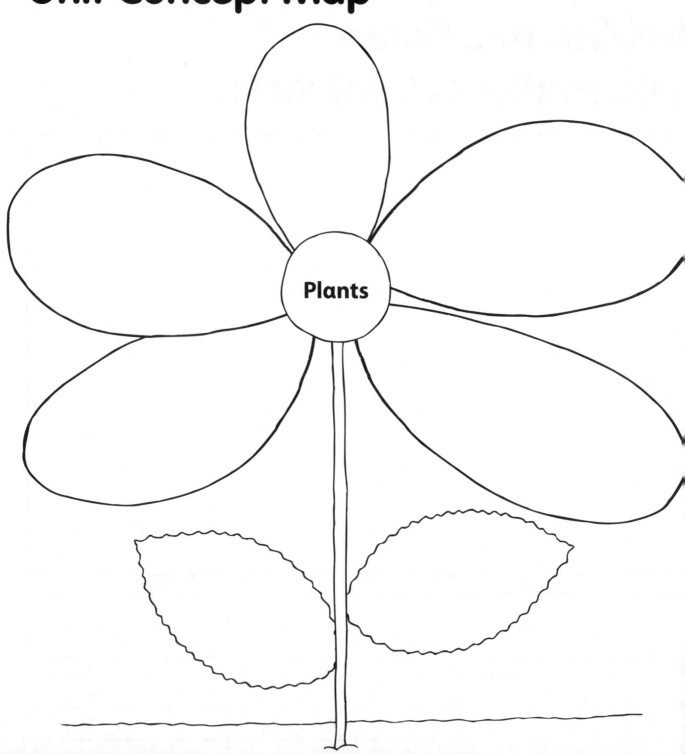

Plants

Directions: Have children write plant names, or draw or glue pictures of plants in the petals and leaves of the concept map.

Our Garden

Directions: Have children find each fruit and vegetable in the garden and color it. Then have one partner point to a fruit or vegetable while the other partner names it.

Name _____

Cause	Effect

→

Directions: Have children draw pictures of something that happens in *Princess Petunia and the Pea* in the left box (a cause) and then draw a picture of its effect in the right box.

For use with TE p. T307   **4.3**   **Unit 4** | All Kinds of Plant·

Vocabulary

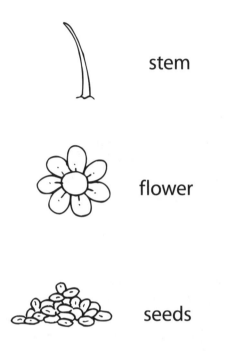

stem

flower

seeds

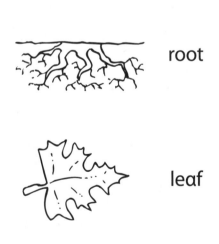

root

leaf

trunk

Directions: Have children color the pictures. Then have children draw a line from each plant part on the left to the corresponding part on the plants at right. Have partners take turns naming the parts of each plant.

Vocabulary

Action Words

Directions: Have children color the page. Then have them play a game with their partner. Have one partner act out the actions. The other partner guesses the action.

For use with TE p. T336

4.5

Unit 4 | All Kinds of Plant

Writing

Beginning

Middle

End

This is _____ .

_____ .

_____ .

Directions: Have children draw pictures in the boxes to show a story. Then help them write the events.

Name _____

Compare Fairy Tales

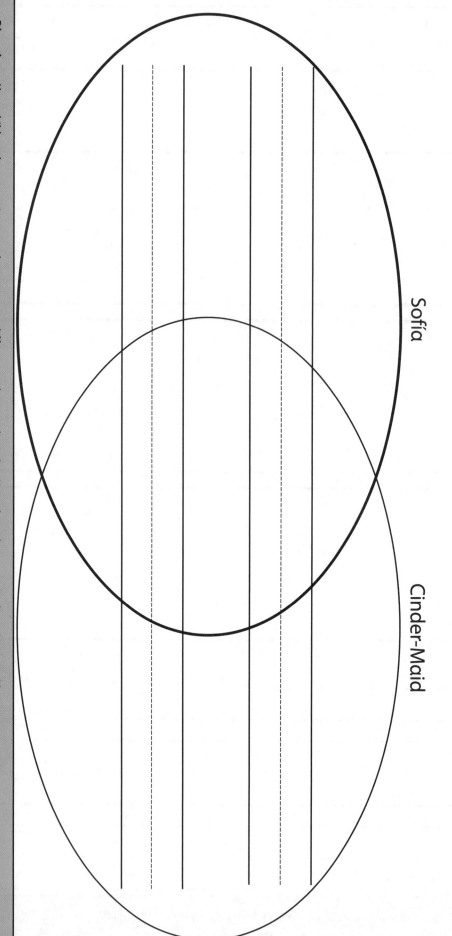

Sofia

Cinder-Maid

Directions: Have children draw or write ways the stories are different in the outside circles. Have them draw or write how they are alike in the overlapping section.

For use with TE p. T345

Name _____

This is _____.

She/He _____.

She/He _____.

She/He _____.

Directions: Have children draw pictures to show what happens in the beginning, middle, and end of in their story. Help them write the story with the frames.

Name _____

Kinds of Plants

bush

vegetable

fruit

tree

Directions: Tell children to color each item a different color: bush, vegetable, fruit, and tree. For example: Color the bush green. Then have them work with a partner. Have one partner say: *Point to the (bush, vegetable, fruit, tree)* while the other partner points.

Title:

_____

_____

Beginning:

_____

_____

_____

_____

Middle:

_____

_____

_____

_____

End:

_____

_____

_____

_____

Unit Concept Map

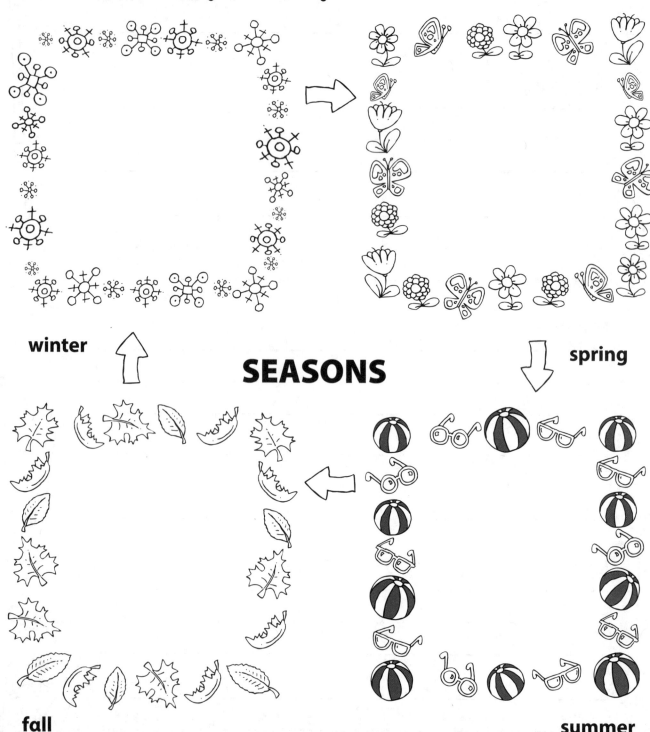

winter

SEASONS

spring

fall

summer

Directions: Have children add their ideas to the concept map.

For use with TE p. T7   **5.1**   **Unit 5** | Wind, Rain, and Snow

Clothing Words

Directions: Review clothing words: *pants, sandals, umbrella, hat, jacket, raincoat, shorts, scarf, shirt, boots.* Then have children color each piece of clothing a specific color. For example: *Color the umbrella yellow. Color the boots red.*

Name _____

Interpret Visuals

```
┌─────────────────────────┐     ┌─────────────────────────┐
│                         │     │                         │
│                         │     │                         │
│                         │     │                         │
│                         │     │                         │
│                         │     │                         │
└─────────────────────────┘     └─────────────────────────┘
- - - - - - - - - - - - - -     - - - - - - - - - - - - - -
_____       _____
```

┌───┐
│   **Bears and the Seasons**   │
└───┘

```
┌─────────────────────────┐     ┌─────────────────────────┐
│                         │     │                         │
│                         │     │                         │
│                         │     │                         │
│                         │     │                         │
│                         │     │                         │
└─────────────────────────┘     └─────────────────────────┘
- - - - - - - - - - - - - -     - - - - - - - - - - - - - -
_____       _____
```

Directions: Have children draw details about each season in *Bears and the Seasons*. Have them write the name of each season under the appropriate box.

Name _____

Seasons

fall

summer

spring

winter

Directions: Have children color the pictures. Read each season word. Then have children draw a line to match the name of the season to the picture. Repeat for all season words. Then name a season and have children act out putting on the appropriate clothing.

Weather Words

sunny

snowy

windy

rainy

Directions: Have children look at each pair of pictures. Read the word beside each pair. Have children circle the picture that matches the weather word. Then have them color the pictures.

Name _____

Writing

Plan a Poem

I see _____ .

I see _____ .

It is _____ .

I see _____ .

I see _____ .

I like _____ .

Directions: Help children choose a season and write it in the center circle. Then have them draw pictures that show what they see in that season. Help them complete the sentence frames.

Name _____

Compare Photo Essays

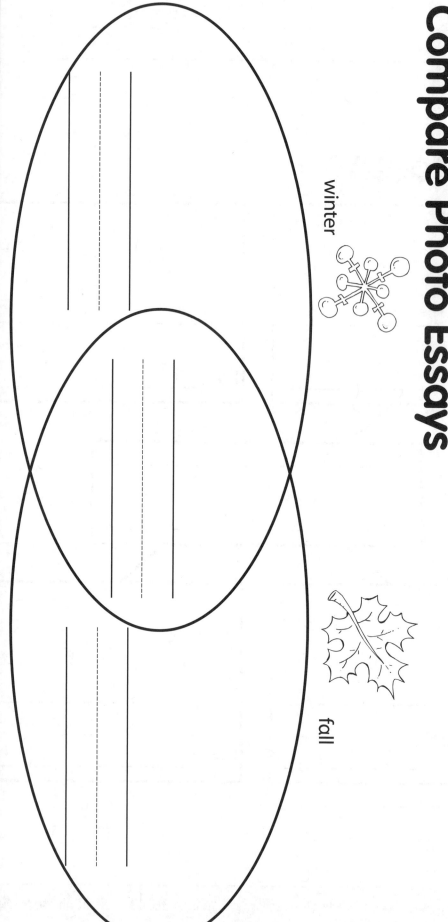

winter

fall

Directions: Talk with children about how winter and fall are alike. List their ideas. Have children choose one idea to copy in the middle of the diagram. Then talk about how they are different. Have children draw or write something unique about each season in its corresponding circle.

5.7

Unit 5 | Wind, Rain, and Snow

Name _____

Writing

Draft a Poem

_____

Title _____

It is _____.

It is _____.

I see _____.

It is _____.

I like _____.

Directions: Have children draw a picture for their poem on a separate sheet of paper. Then have them use their webs from Day 2 to complete the sentence frames in the poem.

Name _____

Sense Words

taste

hear

see

touch

smell

Directions: Read the first sense word: *taste*. Ask children *What do we use to taste?* (our mouth) Have children draw a line from the word to the picture. Repeat for the other sense words. Then have children color the pictures.

Name _____

Title _____

It is _____ .

It is _____ .

I see _____ .

It is _____ .

I like _____ .

Directions: Have children copy their poems. Remind them to leave a little space between letters and more space between words.

Name _____

Unit Concept Map

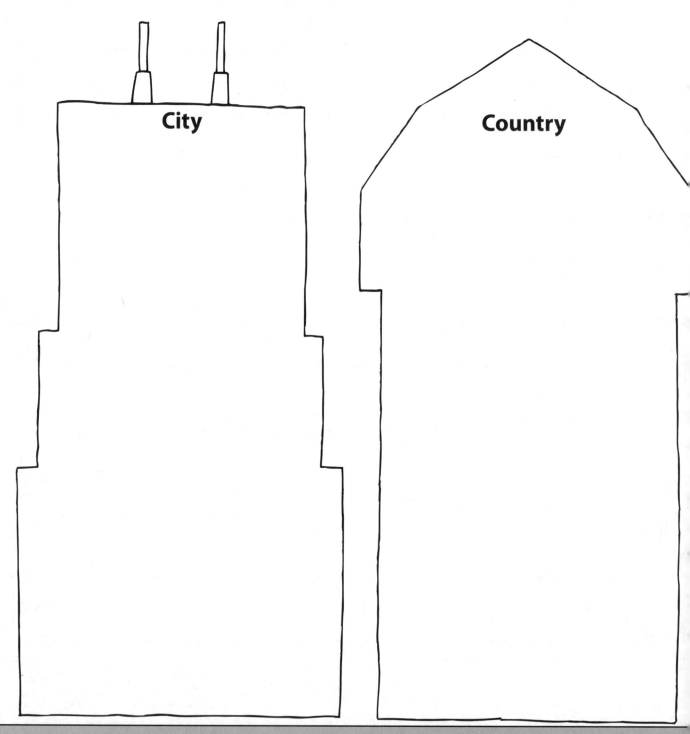

City

Country

Directions: Have children draw pictures or write words related to the city and country.

Name _____

Shopping List Words

bananas
cereal
bread
sandwich
soup
cake

shoes
socks
sandals
shorts

Directions: Have children color the pictures. Then have them draw a circle around things they can eat and draw a box around things they can wear.

Name _____

Fox

Both

Crow

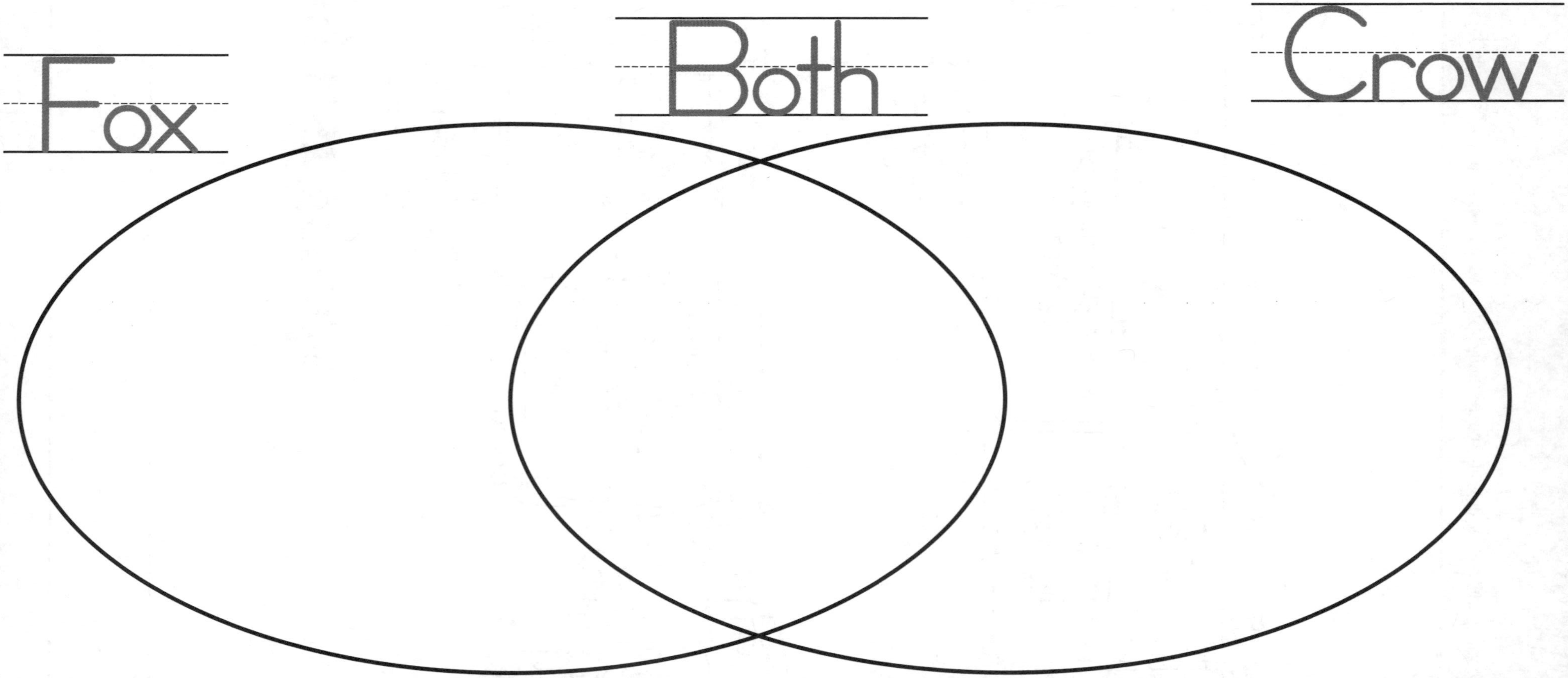

Directions: Have children draw and write to show how Fox and Crow are alike and different.

For use with TE p. T123

6.3

Unit 6 | It's Our Town

Name _____

Community Places

post office
bakery

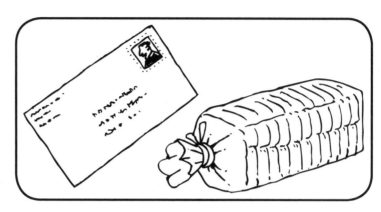

library
grocery store

restaurant
store

Directions: Have children color the items in the boxes. Read the first word in each pair and have students draw a circle around the object that can be found there. Then read the second word in each pair and have students draw a line under the object that can be found in that place.

Name

Safety Words

crosswalk   stop sign   traffic light   walk   look

Directions: Have children color the street scene. Then have partners describe the scene. Encourage them to use the safety words they have learned.

Writing

Plan a Letter

```
┌─────────────────────────────────────────────┐
│                                               │
│                                               │
│                                               │
└─────────────────────────────────────────────┘
        ┌───────────────┼───────────────┐
┌─────────┐     ┌─────────┐     ┌─────────┐
│         │     │         │     │         │
│         │     │         │     │         │
│         │     │         │     │         │
└─────────┘     └─────────┘     └─────────┘
```

I visited the _____ .

It was _____ .

I liked _____ .

Directions: Have children draw a picture or write the name of a place they visited in the top box. Then help them draw pictures or write words in the bottom boxes to name the person they will write to, tell how the visit was, and tell what they liked.

Name _____

Compare Fables

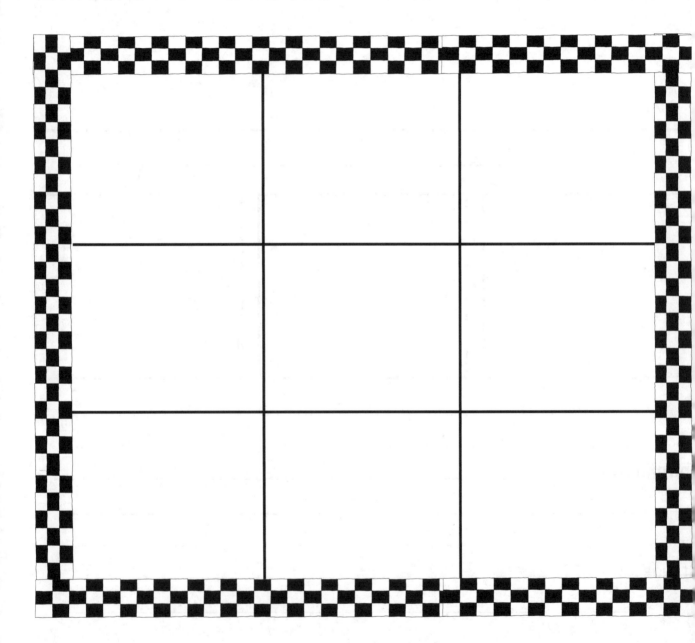

Directions: Have pairs draw pictures in the middle column to show how the fables are alike. Have them draw pictures in each story's column to show how they are different. Have pairs share their charts.

Draft a Letter

_____

_____

_____

Dear ------------------------------------

_____

_____

My class visited the _____ .

_____

----

t was _____ .

_____

----

liked _____ .

Thank you,

_____

_____

Directions: *Day 3* Help children draft their letters. Remind them to use their main idea diagrams from **Practice Master 6.6**.
Day 4 Have children revise their letters to make sure all details were included. Have partners edit their letters. Remind them
to check end punctuation.

Vocabulary

Position Words

in front of		up	
on		over	
above		behind	
down		in	
under		below	

Directions: Have children color the ball in each picture. Say the position word aloud and have children repeat it after you.

_____

_____

_____

Dear _____

_____

_____

I visited the _____

_____

It was _____

_____

I liked _____

Sincerely,

_____

_____

Directions: Have children copy their letters. Remind them to leave a little space between letters and more space between words and to add periods at the end of sentences.

For use with TE p. T169 **6.10** **Unit 6** | It's Our Town

Name _____

Unit Concept Map

JOBS

Directions: Have children add their ideas to the concept map.

Name _____

Jobs

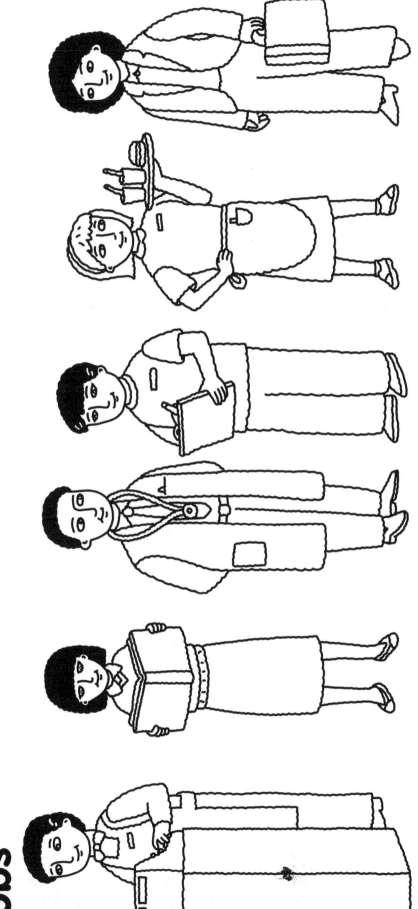

Directions: Have children color the pictures. Then have them point to the corresponding picture as you name each job. Encourage children to act out the jobs.

For use with TE p. T206

7.2

Comprehension

Dr. Nan	Sam

Directions: Have children draw pictures and write labels to show the ways that Dr. Nan helped people in the left column. Then have them draw pictures and write labels to show the ways that Sam helped people in the right column.

Places to Work

restaurant

bank

office building

hospital

school

shopping center

Directions: Review each workplace. Name a job and have children point to where a person in that career might work. Then have children color the pictures and circle the places they have seen.

Vocabulary

Money

penny 1¢

dime 5¢

dollar  10¢

nickel 25¢

quarter  100¢

Directions: Review money words with children. Then review the amounts in each coin and in a dollar. Help children match the coins and dollar on the left to the correct amount on the right. Then display real coins. Have children put the coins in the same order as the coins shown on the bottom of the page.

Name _____

Plan a Fact Book

RESEARCH

Where?

What?

A _____ works at a _____ .

A _____ .

Directions: Review research resources in the box at the top. Then have children complete the web with where the person works and what the person does. Encourage them to use the information in the web to complete the sentence frames.

Comprehension

Directions: Review the types of media in "Help Wanted." Guide children to identify media that is printed and media that is delivered through technology. Have them draw pictures of each type in the appropriate columns. Then discuss other types of media they know (books, commercials on television).

Name _____

Draft a Fact Book

_____

Job: _____

Job: _____

_____   _____

A _____ works in a _____ .

_____   _____

A _____   _____ .

Directions: *Day 3* Have children write the name of the job from their idea web on the first line. Tell children to draw a picture of the person working. Guide children to use the sentence frames to write facts. *Day 4* Have children revise their fact books to include any information they left out. Remind them to edit for subject-verb agreement.

Vocabulary

Job Actions

| teach | learn | help | work | listen |

Directions: Read aloud each word in the box. Have children use crayons to circle each word in a different color as you say it. Have children find who is teaching, learning, etc. and circle the action in the picture with the corresponding color.

Name ____________________

Writing

Job: ____________________

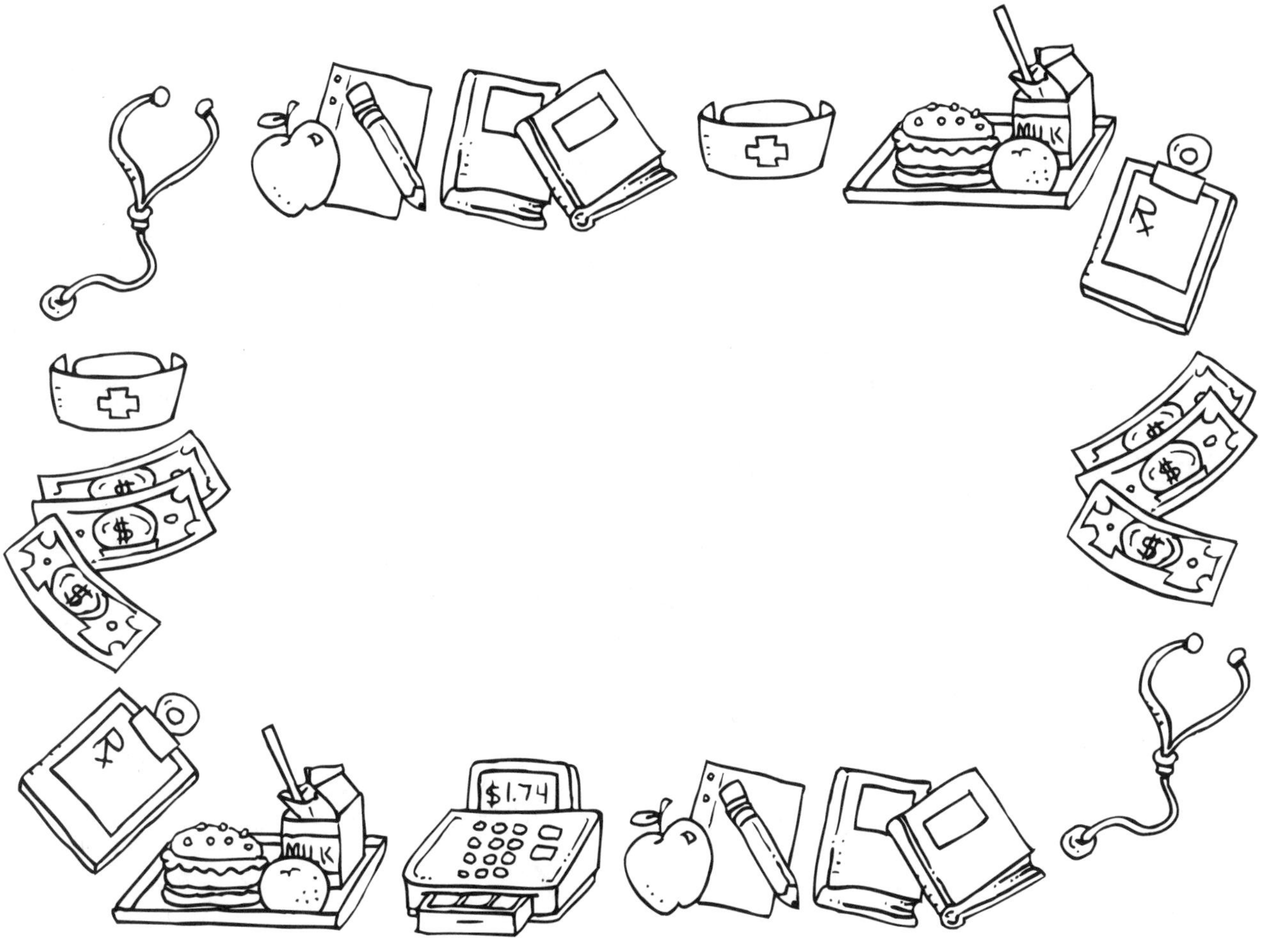

A __________ works in a ____________________.

A ____________________ ____________________.

Directions: Have children copy their fact book. Remind them to leave a little space between letters and more space between words.

Name _____

Unit Concept Map

Directions: Have children add their ideas to the concept map.

Sky Words

cloud

planet

moon

sun

star

Directions: Have children color the pictures. Read aloud the first word: *cloud*. Then have children draw a line from the word to the correct picture. Repeat for the remaining words and pictures.

Name _____

Write Rhymes

dog   bike   mouse   cat

Word	Rhyming Word
house	_____
log	_____
hat	_____
like	_____

Directions: Read the words to children. Have children write rhyming words from the word bank in the T chart.

Name _____

Time

morning

noon

clock

night

calendar

January

day

Directions: Have children color the page. Then have partners discuss other activities they like to do during these time periods.

Vocabulary

The Sun Moves

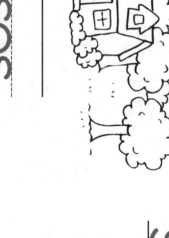

rises

shines

sets

Directions: Have children color the sun in each picture. Then have partners use the pictures to take turns telling how the sun moves in the sky.

Writing

Plan a Story

Beginning

It is _____ .

↓

Middle

_____ sees _____ .

↓

End

_____ .

Directions: Have children draw a picture for each part of their story in each box. Then help them complete the sentence frames.

Name _____

Compare Lullabies

Alike	Different

Directions: Guide children through completing each part of the graphic organizer. Have children write or draw to show ways that the lullabies "New Moon" and "Bells Are Ringing" are alike and different.

For use with TE p. T345

8.7

Unit 8 | Sun, Moon, Stars Above

Draft a Story

Title _____

by _____

It is _____ .

_____ _____

_____ sees _____ .

_____

_____

_____ .

Directions: *Day* 3 Help children draft their stories. Remind them to use their story maps from **Practice Master 8.6**. *Day 4* Have children revise their stories. Have partners edit their stories. Remind them to check end punctuation.

Describing Words

Directions: Say the following sentences with key words. Have children point to the corresponding picture. Say: *Point to something that is round.* Then say: *Point to the picture that shows it is early.* Repeat using the words *bright, dark, low, high,* and *late.* Then have children color the pictures.

Title _____

_____

_____

by _____

_____

It is _____ .

_____ _____

_____ sees _____ .

_____

_____ .

_____

_____ .

Directions: Have children copy their stories. Remind them to leave a little space between letters and more space between words.

For use with TE p. T353   **8.10**   **Unit 8** | Sun, Moon, Stars Above

Tool for School!

_____

Here is _____ tool for school!

_____

_____ 's Book

_____

Here is _____ pair of scissors.

_____

Here is _____ book.

Here is _____ pencil.

Here is _____ block.

Here is _____ crayon.

Here is _____ bottle of glue.

A Great First Day!

_____

_____ 's Book

In the Classroom

I use many things in

_____

_____ classroom.

_____

_____ 's Book

1

I use _____ glue.

I use _____ books.

3

_____
- - - - - - - - - - - - - - - - - - -
2   I use _____ pencils.

_____
- - - - - - - - - - - - - - - - - - -
I use _____ crayons.

_____
- - - - - - - - - - - - - - - - - - -
I use _____ blocks.

4

_____
- - - - - - - - - - - - - - - - - - -
I use _____ scissors.

_____

_____ is the school!

This Place

_____

_____ 's Book

✂

_____

_____ is the playground.

_____
----
is the office.

_____

----

2 _____ is the classroom.

_____

_____ is the bus stop.

_____

_____ is the bathroom.

_____

_____ is the lunch room.

4

Where **I**s it?

It _____ at school!

_____ 's Book

It _____ on the playground.

It _____ in the classroom.

2 It _____ in the office.

It _____ at the bus stop.

It _____ in the lunch room.

It _____ in the bathroom.

4

_____

_____ is this?

_____

_____ 's Book

1

_____

_____ is this?

_____

_____ is this?

3

_____
- - - - - - - - - - - - - - - - -
_____   is this?

_____
- - - - - - - - - - - - - - - - -
_____   is this?

2

_____
- - - - - - - - - - - - - - - - -
_____   is this?

_____
- - - - - - - - - - - - - - - - -
_____   is this?

4

Tab and Her Family

_____

_____ 's Book

✂

2

4

_____

This is _____ family.

This Is
My Family

_____

_____ 's Book

✂ 1

_____

This is _____ sister.

_____

This is _____ father.

3

_____

This is _____ mother.

_____

This is _____ brother.

_____

This is _____ grandma.

_____

This is _____ grandpa.

_____

_____ can do many things!

She Can!

_____

_____ 's Book

_____

_____ can laugh.

_____

_____ can sing.

_____

_____ can cook.

_____ can eat.

2

_____

_____ can dance.

_____

_____ can play.

4

How does _____ feel?

How Does

He Feel?

_____

_____ 's Book

✂ 1

_____ is excited.

_____ is angry.

3

_____

_____ is bored.

2

_____

_____ is sad.

_____

_____ is happy.

_____

_____ is surprised.

4

_____
- - - - - - - - - - - - - - -
_____ see the farm!

_____
- - - - - - - - - - - - - - -
_____ 's Book

1

✂ -

_____
- - - - - - - - - - - - - - -
_____ see a pig.

_____
- - - - - - - - - - - - - - -
_____ see a cow.

3

_____

_____ see a goose.

2

_____

_____ see a horse.

_____

_____ see a chicken.

4

_____

_____ see a sheep.

The Singing Donkey

_____

- -

_____ 's Book

_____

I _____ farm animals.

I  Animals!

_____

_____'s Book

_____

I _____ white sheep.

_____

I _____ pink pigs.

_____

2   I _____   fast horses.

_____

I _____   yellow chickens.

_____

I _____   brown cows.

_____

I _____   noisy geese.

4

_____

_____ is a farm?

_____

_____ 's Book

1

_____

_____ is a lamb?

_____

_____ is a foal?

3

_____

_____   is a piglet?

2

(top right)

_____

_____   is a chick?

_____

_____   is a duckling?

_____

_____   is a calf?

4

_____

The horse _____ a baby!

_____

_____ 's Book

1

✂

_____

The horse _____ feet.

_____

The horse _____ a head.

3

2 The horse _____ a tail.

The horse _____ a nose.

The horse _____ ears.

The horse _____ legs.

4

Here is a basket of fruits

_____

_____ vegetables. Yum!

_____

_____ 's Book

1

Here is a strawberry

_____

_____ an orange.

Here is a peach

_____

_____ a carrot.

3

Here is an apple

_____

_____ a bean.

Here is a banana

_____

_____ a pepper.

Here is a pear

_____

_____ an onion.

Here is a potato

_____

_____ a tomato.

Princess Petunia and the Pea

_____

- -

_____ 's Book

1

2

4

_____

_____ is my plant!

It Is
My Plant!

_____

_____ 's Book

1

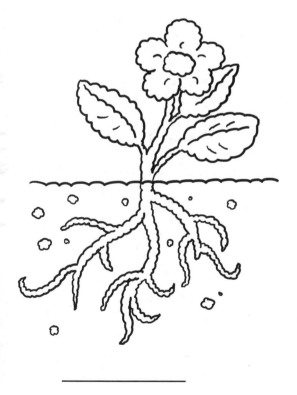

_____

_____ has a flower.

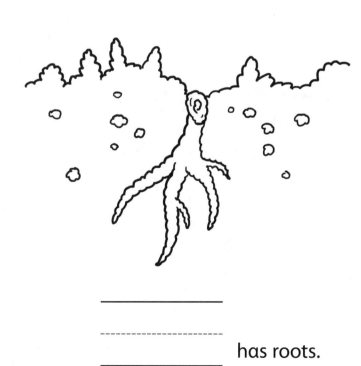

_____

_____ has roots.

3

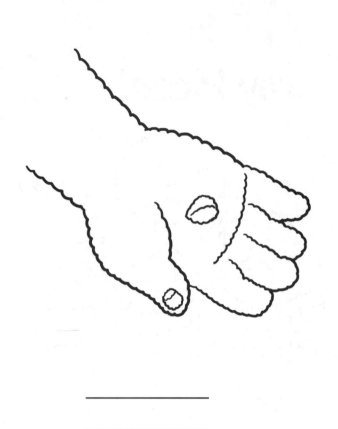

_____

_____ is small.

2

_____

_____ gets bigger.

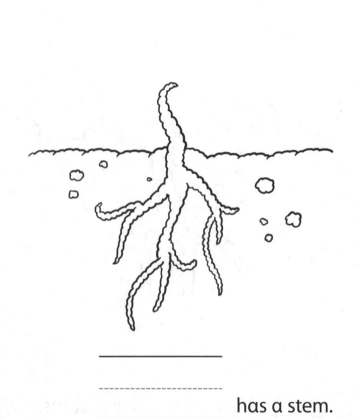

_____

_____ has a stem.

_____

_____ has a leaf.

_____

_____ eat the soup!

You Grow a Garden!

_____

_____ 's Book

1

_____

_____ pick carrots.

_____

_____ plant.

3

_____

_____ dig.

2

_____

_____ put carrots in the sou

_____

_____ water.

_____

_____ grow carrots.

4

_____

- - - - - - - - - - - - - - - -

I _____ go to market!

I Can
Go to Market!

_____

- - - - - - - - - - - - - - - -

_____ 's Book

1

_____

- - - - - - - - - - - - - - - -

_____ put them in a box.

_____

- - - - - - - - - - - - - - - -

I _____ pick them from a plant.

3

_____

I _____ pick vegetables.

_____

I _____ put food in the truc[k]

2

_____

I _____ pick fruit.

_____

I _____ pick them from a tr[ee]

4

Give Him a Jacket!

_____
----
him sandals!

_____

's Book

_____
----
him a hat!

_____
----
him boots!

_____

2 _____ him an umbrella!

_____

_____ him a scarf!

_____

_____ him pants!

_____

_____ him a jacket!

Bears and the Seasons

_____

_____

_____ 's Book

✂ 1

2

4

Share with _____ .

Share with

Him !

_____ 's Book

Talk with _____ .

Eat with _____ .

Sit with _____ .

Read with _____ .

Play with _____ .

Laugh with _____ .

We like the weather!

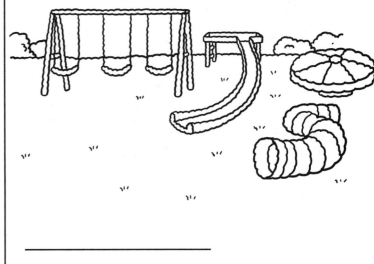

Do You Like the Weather?

_____
- - - - - - - - - - - - - - - - - -
_____ 's Book

1

✂

_____
- - - - - - - - - - - - - - - - - -
_____ you like hot weather?

_____
- - - - - - - - - - - - - - - - - -
_____ you like snowy weather?

3

_____

2 _____ you like windy weather?

_____

_____ you like the weather?

_____

_____ you like cold weather?

_____

_____ you like rainy weather?

4

I Like It, Too

I like you.

_____

I like you, _____ !

_____

_____ 's Book

✂ 1

I like winter snow.

I like it, _____ !

3

I like the summer sun.

_____
- - - - - - - - - - - - - - - - - - - -
I like it, _____ !

I like spring flowers.

_____
- - - - - - - - - - - - - - - - - - - -
I like them, _____ !

_____

I _____ good food.

I Get Food

_____

_____ 's Book

✂

_____

I _____ cereal.

_____

I _____ bread.

_____

I _____ bananas.

_____

I _____ a sandwich.

2

_____

I _____ soup.

_____

I _____ cake.

4

Fox and Crow

_____
- -
_____ 's Book

1

3

This Is Her Day

_____
- - - - - - - - - - - - - - - - -
_____ 's Book

_____
- - - - - - - - - - - - - - - - -
She sees _____ family!

_____
- - - - - - - - - - - - - - - - -
She gets _____ bread.

_____
- - - - - - - - - - - - - - - - -
She gets _____ letters.

_____

She eats _____ cereal.

2

_____

She gets _____ bananas.

_____

She gets _____ shoes.

4

_____

She eats _____ sandwich.

Where

Is My Dog?

_____

_____ is my dog?

_____

_____ 's Book

1

_____

_____ is my dog?

_____

_____ is my dog?

3

_____

----

2 _____ is my dog?

_____

_____ is my dog?

_____

_____ is my dog?

_____

_____ is my dog?

4

Yes, he is home!

Is Sam Home?

No

_____

_____ 's Book

1

✂

_____ , he is in the grocery store.

_____ , he is in the lunch room.

_____
- - - - - - - - - - - - - - -
_____ , he is in the classroom.

2

_____
- - - - - - - - - - - - - - -
_____ , he is in the bakery.

_____
- - - - - - - - - - - - - - -
_____ , he is in the library.

_____
- - - - - - - - - - - - - - -
_____ , he is in the post office.

4

My teacher _____ here.

My Teacher
<u>Goes</u> Here

_____'s Book

1

My teacher _____ here.

My teacher _____ here.

3

_____

My teacher _____ here.

2

_____

My teacher _____ here.

_____

My teacher _____ here.

_____

My teacher _____ here.

4

Sam and Mom at Work

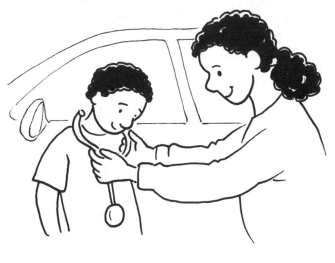

_____

- - - - - - - - - - - - - - - - - -

_____ 's Book

 1

2

4

They go _____ work.

They Go _____ to Work

_____ 's Book

✂ -

He goes _____ work.

She goes _____ work.

2

He goes _____ work.

She goes _____ work.

He goes _____ work.

She goes _____ work.

4

_____
- - - - - - - - - - - - - - -
I _____ to be me!

_____
- - - - - - - - - - - - - - - - - - -
_____ 's Book

1

_____
- - - - - - - - -
I _____ to be a waiter.

_____
- - - - - - - - -
I _____ to be a banker.

3

_____

2   I _____ to be a doctor.

_____

I _____ to be a teacher.

_____

I _____ to be a cashier.

_____

I _____ to be a nurse.

4

What will you _____ ?

_____ 's Book

1

What will we _____ ?

What will she _____ ?

3

_____

What will I _____ ?

_____

What will she _____ ?

2

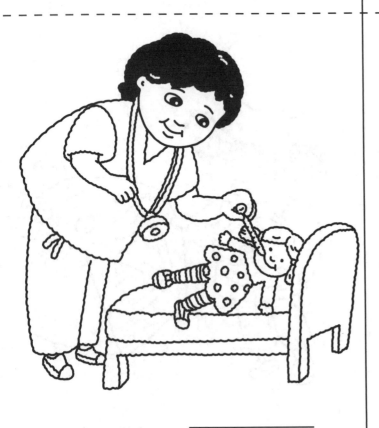

_____

What will she _____ ?

_____

What will they _____ ?

4

_____

What will I _____ tomorrow?

I See

the Sky

_____

_____'s Book

_____

I _____ a planet.

_____

I _____ clouds .

2

I _____ the sun.

I _____ the sky.

I _____ the moon.

I _____ stars.

4

Baby Mouse Goes to Bed

_____

- - - - - - - - - - - - - - - - - - - -

_____ 's Book

1

✂

3

2

4

ke the day,

_____

- - - - - - - - - - -

_____   I like the night, too.

Morning and Night

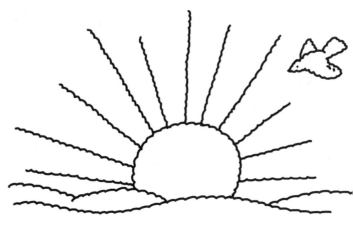

_____

- - - - - - - - - - -

_____   's Book

1

_____

- - - - - - - - - - -

aw in the morning,   _____

I listen to stories at night.

I eat cereal in the morning,

_____

- - - - - - - - - - -

_____   I eat soup at night.

3

I wake up in the morning,

 I sleep at night.

2

I am loud in the morning,

_____

_____

I am quiet at night.

I ride my bike in the morning,

_____

_____

I walk at night.

4

I go to school in the morning,

_____

_____

I come home at nigh

_____

- - - - - - - - - - - - -

_____ see the sun set.

_____

- - - - - - - - - - - - -

_____ 's Book

1

✂ -

_____

- - - - - - - - - - - - -

_____ see clouds.

_____

- - - - - - - - - - - - -

_____ see the moon.

3

_____

_____ see stars.

2

_____

_____ see the sun shine.

_____

_____ see a planet.

_____

_____ see the sun rise.

4

What __A__re They?

They _____ stars.

_____ 's Book

They _____ high.

They _____ planets.

They _____ round.

They _____ bright.

They _____ dark.

They _____ clouds.

Vocabulary

Unit 1 Vocabulary

School Tools	Actions	School Places	Commands
black scissors	build	bathroom	ask
blue crayon	draw	bus stop	bring
green block	make	classroom	point
red book	read	lunch room	sit
white glue	run	office	share
yellow pencil	write	playground	stand

High Frequency Words

a

is

the

this

Language Frames

a _____

the _____

1.21

Vocabulary

Unit 2 Vocabulary

Family	Food	Feelings	Actions
baby	pizza	angry	cook
brother	fish	bored	eat
father	rice	excited	dance
grandma	salad	happy	laugh
grandpa	soup	sad	play
mother	tortillas	surprised	sing
sister			

High Frequency Words

he

my

she

who

Language Frames

Who is this? This is my _____

She/He is _____

Vocabulary

Unit 3 Vocabulary

Farm Animals	Describing Words	Baby Animals	Animal Parts
chicken	big	calf	ears
cow	fast	chick	feet
duck	little	duckling	head
goat	loud	foal	legs
goose	quiet	gosling	nose
horse	slow	kid	tail
pig		lamb	wings
sheep		piglet	

High Frequency Words

has

I

like

what

Language Frames

I like the _____.

This _____ is _____.

What has a _____? A has a _____.

Vocabulary

Unit 4 Vocabulary

Fruits and Vegetables	Plant Parts	Plants	Actions
apple pear	flower	bush	dig
bean pepper	leaf	fruit	grow
carrot potato	root	tree	pick
onion tomato	seed	vegetable	plant
peach	stem		put
	trunk		water

High Frequency Words

and

can

it

you

Language Frames

That is a _____. It has a _____ and a _____.

You can _____ the _____. I can _____ the _____.

Vocabulary

Unit 5 Vocabulary

Clothing	Seasons	Weather Words	Sense Words
boots scarf	fall	rain/rainy	hear
hat shirt	spring	snow/snowy	see
jacket shorts	summer	sunshine/sunny	smell
pants	winter	wind/windy	taste
sandals			touch
raincoat			
umbrella			

High Frequency Words

do

give

him

too

Language Frames

It is _____. Give him a _____.

I _____ the _____.

I like _____. Do you like _____. too?

5.21

Vocabulary

Unit 6 Vocabulary

Shopping List Words		Community Places	Safety Words	Position Words	
bananas	shoes	bakery	crosswalk	above	on
bread	shorts	grocery store	look	behind	over
cake	socks	library	stop sign	below	under
cereal	soup	post office	traffic light	down	up
sandals		restaurant	walk	in	
sandwich		store		in front of	

High Frequency Words

get

her

no

where

Language Frames

This is a _____. She can get her _____.

Where is he? Is he _____ the _____?

No, he is _____ the _____.

Name _____

Unit 7 Vocabulary

Kinds of Jobs	Places to Work	Job Actions	Money Words
banker	bank	help	dime
cashier	hospital	learn	dollar
doctor	office building	listen	money
nurse	restaurant	teach	nickel
teacher	school	work	penny
waiter	shopping center		quarter

High Frequency Words

be

goes

to

want

Language Frames

This is a _____. _____ goes to a _____.

I like to _____. I want to be a _____.

Unit 8 Vocabulary

Objects in the Sky	Time	Describing Words	
cloud	calendar	bright	move
moon	clock	dark	rises
planet	day	early	round
star	morning	high	sets
sun	night	late	shines
	noon	low	

High Frequency Words

are

but

see

they

Language Frames

It is _____. I see the _____, but I do not see the _____.

See the _____. They are _____.

Name

Alphabet

TIONAL
GRAPHIC
RNING

CENGAGE
Learning°

Acknowledgments

Grateful acknowledgment is given to the authors, artists, photographers, museums, publishers, and agents for permission to reprint copyrighted material. Every effort has been made to secure the appropriate permission. If any omissions have been made or if corrections are required, please contact the Publisher.

Cover Illustration: Joel Sotelo

Please see the Level A Reach Student Book for all image acknowledgments.

For product information and technology assistance, contact us at
Customer & Sales Support, 888-915-3276

For permission to use material from this text or product, submit all requests online at **www.cengage.com/permissions**
Further permissions questions can be emailed to
permissionrequest@cengage.com

National Geographic Learning | Cengage Learning
1 Lower Ragsdale Drive
Building 1, Suite 200
Monterey, CA 93940

Cengage Learning is a leading provider of customized learning solutions with office locations around the globe, including Singapore, the United Kingdom, Australia, Mexico, Brazil, and Japan. Locate your local office at **www.cengage.com/global**.

Visit National Geographic Learning online at **NGL.Cengage.com**
Visit our corporate website at **www.cengage.com**

ISBN: 978-1-3371-0988-8 (Practice Book)

ISBN: 978-1-3371-0994-9 (Practice Masters)
Teachers are authorized to reproduce the practice masters in this book in limited quantity and solely for use in their own classrooms.

Printed in the USA.
Globus Printing & Packaging, Inc.
Minster, OH

Print Number: 03

Print Year: 2020